CAN'T I JUST

Get it Together?

How to Handle People, Problems, and Everything They Didn't Teach You in School

Jennifer Larsen

Originality Statement

This book is an original work written by the author and reflects their unique ideas, voice, and instructional approach. While it may reference common educational and career-planning concepts, all content, including structure, language, exercises, and framework, is the author's own creation. Any similarities to other published works are purely coincidental.

Printed in the United States of America

ISBN: 978-1-968756-81-9

First Edition

Cover design by Rachel Bostwick

Interior design and layout by Rachel Bostwick

For information or bulk orders, visit cantijust.com

Contents

 **INTRODUCTION:**
So You're Supposed to Be an Adult
Now… (And You're Still Not Sure
Where the Hell That Manual Is)…

Let's be honest: adulting didn't come with instructions.

One day you're supposed to know how to feed yourself, clean a bathroom, juggle appointments, email your boss, answer the phone like a real human, and somehow also budget, network, manage your emotions, and not look like you're panicking in meetings.

And if you missed the memo on all that? It's not your fault.

This book is here for the people who feel like they're **faking it every day** and hoping no one notices.

What This Book Is

This is a *practical, kind, no-judgment guide* to:

- Getting through daily life without falling apart

- Talking to people at work without setting off awkward alarms

- Managing time, money, messes, and misunderstandings

- Handling feedback, meetings, and panic-texting your friend to reread an email you already sent

- Feeling like a functional adult, even if you're still figuring things out

It's a crash course in soft skills and life skills—**the stuff you were expected to know, but maybe never learned.**

What This Book Is Not

- A lecture

- A perfection checklist

- A fake-it-till-you-make-it hustle guide

- A "just be more confident!" motivational speech in disguise

This isn't about changing who you are. It's about **learning the rules of the world** so you can work with them—not get wrecked by them.

Who This Is For

This book is for:

- Neurodivergent adults who feel like they missed a social or organizational download

- Late bloomers who were busy surviving while everyone else was "growing up"

- Anxious overthinkers, awkward job-seekers, and "functioning humans" who still microwave their dinner while sitting on the floor in the dark

- Anyone who wants to get their life together but doesn't know where to start

If that's you: **you're in the right place.**

You're not behind. You're not failing. You just need a little help, and that's not a flaw—it's smart.

Read This However You Need

You don't have to read this book front to back. You can skip around. Jump to the chapter that's stressing you out the most. Read one section. Take a break. Come back in a week.

There's no grade. No deadline. No quiz.

Just real tools, real talk, and a steady reminder that *you're not the only one trying to figure this out*.

So take a breath. You're not broken. You're not alone.

Let's get into it—one skill, one page, one totally manageable grown-up moment at a time.

CHAPTER 1:
Feeding Yourself Without Fire Hazards
(Or: How to Eat Like an Adult Without Crying in the Grocery Store)

Let's be honest: no one prepared you for the pure chaos of grocery shopping, meal planning, or realizing that you have to feed yourself three times a day every single day forever. That's a lot of decisions – and a lot of dishes.

This chapter is for the people who:

- Get overwhelmed and order takeout again

- Buy random stuff and end up with no actual meals

- Eat cereal for dinner for four nights straight and call it fine (it is, but also: we can level up)

You don't need to be a great cook. You just need to not be starving, broke, or stuck eating sad freezer meals every night. This isn't about impressing anyone – it's about taking care of yourself in the simplest, most doable way.

🔍 Step 1: The Bare-Minimum Food Formula

Here's a dead-simple way to think about meals:

Protein + Carb + Veggie (optional but encouraged) = Meal

- **Protein:** chicken, beans, eggs, tuna, tofu, ground beef, deli meat

- **Carb:** rice, bread, pasta, tortillas, potatoes

- **Veggie:** frozen veggies, salad mix, canned corn, chopped carrots, whatever

You don't need a recipe. Just combine stuff.

Tuna + pasta + frozen peas = meal.
Rice + eggs + spinach = meal.
Tortilla + cheese + beans = meal.

It's not gourmet, but it works – and it beats spending $16 on delivery again.

🛒 Step 2: Buy Ingredients, Not Just Snacks

Here's what happens to a lot of people: they go to the store and fill the cart with snacks, drinks, and microwave meals... but nothing actually goes together.

Try this instead:

- **Pick 3 meals you can make this week**
- Write down what you need for those meals
- Then grab your staples and snacks

If it helps, think of your fridge like a toolbox. Fill it with tools you know how to use.

You don't need a hundred ingredients. But –

DO NOT underestimate the power of sauces.

Seriously. Sauces are the secret weapon of lazy, efficient cooking.

- Chicken + rice + teriyaki sauce = Asian-ish
- Chicken + rice + buffalo sauce = spicy American
- Chicken + rice + pesto = pretend-you're-in-Italy

Same base. Totally different meal. Your brain loves the variety.

Stock a few go-to sauces: soy sauce, buffalo, BBQ, ranch, sriracha, pesto, Caesar – whatever makes your taste buds wake up. They're cheap, they last a while, and they make boring food feel new again.

💧 Step 3: Respect Lazy Cooking

There's no prize for doing it the hard way. Use the shortcuts:

- **Rotisserie chicken:** already cooked, already tasty

- **Microwave rice packets:** done in 90 seconds

- **Bagged salads or frozen veggies:** healthy with zero prep

- **Sheet pan meals:** throw everything on a tray, bake it, eat like a champ

Lazy cooking isn't cheating. It's survival with flair.

Step 4: Don't Fall for the "Should" Voice

You don't need to meal prep five days' worth of quinoa and roasted kale to be "good at adulting." You don't need to go vegan, paleo, keto, or gluten-free unless it actually helps you.

Here's the only food rule that matters:

Eat in a way that makes your body feel okay and your brain not hate you.

That's it. That's the standard.

And if you can't manage a full meal today?

Microwave something. Eat a sandwich. Try again tomorrow.

Feeding yourself at all is a win.

🚜 Bonus Tip: Fast Food Doesn't Have to Be Garbage

There's a myth that every drive-thru meal is a nutritional disaster. But honestly? With a little strategy, you can eat out and still feel good afterward.

Example:
Chick-fil-A's kale salad + grilled nuggets = a legit, balanced meal.

You could eat that every day and not feel gross, broke, or bloated. And it's fast.

Other options to look for:

- Grilled over fried

- Small portions with a healthy side (apple slices > fries sometimes)

- Water or unsweetened tea instead of soda

This isn't about being perfect. It's about finding a few go-to options that won't wreck your energy, your wallet, or your digestion.

Fast food can be fuel – you just have to know what to order.

Quick Start List: Grocery Staples for a Functioning Human

Want to avoid the blank stare in aisle 4? Start here:

- **Proteins:** eggs, rotisserie chicken, canned beans, ground beef, tofu, tuna

- **Carbs:** bread, tortillas, rice, pasta, potatoes

- **Veggies:** frozen broccoli, salad kits, baby carrots, canned corn

- **Sauces:** buffalo, BBQ, soy sauce, pesto, Caesar, sriracha – mix it up!

- **Extras:** olive oil, shredded cheese, peanut butter

- **Snacks:** yogurt, granola bars, popcorn, fruit

If it helps, build a "default grocery list" in your phone. Copy it every week. You're not failing if you eat the same five meals on repeat. That's just called *having a system*.

CHAPTER 2:
Cleaning, Laundry, and Other Witchcraft
(Or: How to Stop Living in a Pile of Your Own Regret)

There's no shame in the mess. Everyone lets things go sometimes. But there's a fine line between *"my place looks lived-in"*
and *"my home feels like a cry for help."* You don't have to become a cleaning wizard – you just need a basic system that
keeps your living space from becoming a biohazard or a mood-
killer.

This chapter is for you if:

- You feel stressed just looking at your space

- You run out of clean clothes regularly

- You've ever used a towel as a napkin and then again as a
  towel (*no judgment*)

Let's break down the basics – what matters, what doesn't, and
how to not drown in it.

Step 1: Lower the Bar – but Keep It Off the Floor

Let's be clear: your space doesn't need to look like a magazine. It just needs to not make you feel gross, stuck, or ashamed. Think *"clean enough to feel okay,"* not *"ready for a white glove inspection."*

Start with this simple rule:

Floors and surfaces. That's it.

If your floor is clear and your surfaces aren't sticky, you're already doing great.

Don't try to overhaul everything in one day. Do a little at a time:

- Pick one corner
- Clear the trash, dishes, clutter
- Wipe it down
- Walk away

One zone at a time. Momentum is more important than perfection.

Step 2: Dishes Are a Mental Health Metric

You don't have to love doing dishes. You just have to not let them stack up to the point of existential crisis. A sink full of dishes makes everything feel worse – more chaotic, more un-manageable, more *"why even bother?"*

The one-dish rule:
Every time you eat, wash that dish. Just one. You don't need to tackle the whole pile – just keep the pile from growing.

If that's too much some days, fine. Soak them in hot water. Come back later. No shame.

Step 3: Laundry Without the Drama

Laundry doesn't have to be a full-day event that ends with your clothes still in the dryer three days later. *(We see you.)*

Here's a lazy but effective system:

- **Sort your laundry once a week** – light, dark, towels

- **Do one load at a time,** from start to finish

- Fold right away *if you can*, but if not?

- Dump it in a clean basket

- Pull out what you need as you go

- Just don't mix it back in with the dirty stuff

And here's a big one:

If it's clean, it's clean. Stop re-washing the same clothes because you forgot to fold them.

You're not failing. You're just a little distracted.

⏱ Step 4: The Five-Minute Reset

Don't wait until things are bad to clean. If you spend just five minutes a day doing a light reset, you'll avoid most mess disasters.

Set a timer. Then:

- Throw away trash

- Wipe one surface

- Put stuff back where it belongs

- Light a candle if you're feeling fancy

And here's the golden rule for neurospicy folks (*and honestly, most humans*):

Don't put it down. Put it away.

If you just drop the mail on the table or your jacket on the chair, your brain will walk away and forget it exists. Then it turns into clutter. But if you take the extra 10 seconds to put it where it actually goes? The task is done. You don't have to remember it later. Future You will thank you.

This tiny ritual tells your brain, *"We live in a place where things are okay."* And that message matters.

Bonus Tip: Clean Space = Clearer Brain

This isn't just about being neat. A cleaner space literally reduces stress. Your environment sends signals to your brain all day long. *Mess says chaos. Clean says "we got this."*

You don't need to turn into someone who loves cleaning. But when your surroundings feel more under control, *you* feel more under control.

That's the whole point of this chapter.

📋 Quick Wins: Cleaning Basics Checklist

If your brain loves lists, here's one to start with:

- Wipe down surfaces (kitchen, bathroom, desk)

- Wash dishes (*or at least soak them*)

- Take out the trash

- Sweep or vacuum high-traffic spots

- Do one load of laundry

- Change your sheets (*don't act like you didn't need the reminder*)

- You don't need to do it all today. You just need to do *something.* Then do a little more tomorrow.

🖌 This isn't witchcraft. It's maintenance.

CHAPTER 3:
Time, Tasks, and "I Forgot Again"
(Or: Why Your Brain is a Dumpster Fire and How to Outsmart It)

If you've ever missed an appointment, spaced on a deadline, or stared at your to-do list like it personally betrayed you, congratulations: you're human. Or maybe neurospicy. Or tired. Or just overwhelmed by the modern miracle that is having 47 things to remember and zero mental energy.

This chapter isn't about becoming some perfectly productive calendar robot. It's about **tricking your brain into helping you –** instead of ghosting you the moment something boring or stressful shows up.

🧠 Step 1: Accept That You Can't Remember Everything

You're not supposed to keep it all in your head. That's not failure – that's biology. Your brain is designed to *notice danger* and *respond emotionally,* not hold a perfectly sorted to-do list at all times.

That's why smart people use tools:

- Calendars

- Timers

- Notes

- Alarms

- Sticky reminders stuck to their forehead if necessary

The goal isn't to become more disciplined. It's to stop trying to carry it all in your head like a hero. Write it down. Put it somewhere you'll actually see it. That's not weakness – it's strategy.

Step 2: Pick One System and Stick to It (Even if It's Ugly)

Do not waste six hours trying to find the perfect planner, app, or color-coded system. You don't need aesthetic. You need something that works with your brain.

Try one of these:

- A digital calendar with alerts (Google Calendar is your free BFF)

- A simple to-do list app (like TickTick, Todoist, or Reminders)

- A notebook with one section for "now," one for "later," and one for "if I have energy"

- A giant whiteboard on the wall, if you're visual and easily distracted

Whichever system you choose – **keep using it even if it's messy**. The goal isn't perfection. It's completion.

✎ Step 3: Break the Task Until It's So Small It's Stupid

Here's why most people procrastinate: the task looks too big. "Clean the apartment." "Do my taxes." "Fix my life."

No one wants to do that.

So break it. Smaller. **No, smaller.**

Not "do laundry." → "Pick up dirty socks."
Not "write paper." → "Open the file."
Not "make appointment." → "Find the phone number."

If you do that one small thing, you're now in motion. That's everything.

⏱ Step 4: Use Time the Way Your Brain Actually Works

Some people can focus for hours. Others need to sneak up on a task like it's a wild animal.

Try these:

- **The 5-minute rule**: Set a timer and work for 5 minutes. If it still sucks, you can stop. (You usually won't.)

- **Body doubling**: Do tasks while someone else is nearby – online or in person. Doesn't matter if they're doing their own thing. It keeps you grounded.

- **Habit stacking**: Tie new tasks to existing habits. "I'll check my planner after I brush my teeth." "I'll take out the trash when I grab coffee."

Work with your brain. Not against it.

🔁 Bonus Tip: Late Doesn't Mean Lost

Maybe you missed the deadline. Forgot to text back. Slept through something important.

You don't need to spiral. You just need to restart.

- Apologize if needed.

- Do the thing late anyway.

- Set a reminder for next time.

Being late doesn't make you bad. It just makes you human.

Quick Wins: Task-Taming Cheat Sheet

- Set phone alarms for *everything* – even little things

- Keep a pen and notebook by your bed, your bag, or your toilet (no judgment)

- Use visual cues – put your meds next to your toothbrush, your lunch by your keys

- Celebrate every tiny win: "I emailed the dentist!" = Victory

- Don't wait to feel motivated. Just get moving. Action creates motivation – not the other way around

You're not lazy. You're overloaded.

You don't need discipline. You need systems that support your real life.

Let's build them.

CHAPTER 4:

Money Isn't Magic. It's Math (But Easy Math)

(Or: How to Not Be Broke Without Being Bored to Death)

Here's the secret nobody wants to say out loud: a lot of financially struggling people aren't dumb or irresponsible. They're just trying to survive without a clear map. They were never taught the rules, and now they're expected to play the game.

This chapter isn't about investing or becoming rich overnight. It's about making sure your money isn't vanishing into the void – and knowing where it goes so you can take the wheel instead of being dragged behind the bumper.

Step 1: Know What's Coming In and What's Going Out

That's the whole deal.

Money in > Money out = Stability
Money out > Money in = Stress

You don't need a perfect budget, but you do need a snapshot of your life:

- **How much do you make?** *(after taxes, not before)*

- **What are your fixed expenses?** *(rent, phone, subscriptions, gas, etc.)*

- **What do you spend on extras?** *(food, fun, impulse purchases)*

Once you know those numbers, you can spot where the holes are. You can fix a leak you can see.

Step 2: Pick a Budget System You'll Actually Use

Forget the pretty spreadsheets unless you love that kind of thing. Try one of these:

- **50/30/20 rule:**
    - 50% needs *(bills, groceries, rent)*
    - 30% wants *(fun, eating out, hobby stuff)*
    - 20% savings or paying down debt
- **The Envelope System** *(digital or real envelopes):*
    - Split your money into "buckets" and only spend what's in each one
- **The "look at your bank account once a week and try not to panic" method**
    - Less structured, but still better than nothing

You don't need to track every penny. Just pay attention. That alone can change things.

Step 3: Subscriptions, Snacks, and Sneaky Spending

Some of your money is vanishing without you noticing. Look for:
• Forgotten subscriptions
• Food delivery fees *(those add up fast)*
• Daily "little things" that turn into big things over time

Example: $8 coffee × 5 days a week = $160/month = $1,920/year
That's not judgment – it's just math. If you *love* your coffee, fine!
Just know that you're choosing it, not getting blindsided by it.

If money keeps disappearing, track your spending for a week.
No shame – just info.

Step 3.5: They're Actively Trying to Trick You

This part's important, so let's spell it out:

The system is designed to make you forget you're spending money.

Brightly colored chips in a casino. One-click purchases. Free trials that auto-renew.

They're not accidents. They're features. These tools are built to bypass the part of your brain that says, *"Hey, maybe I can't afford this."*

- **Digital money doesn't feel real** – so you swipe and forget

- **Subscriptions renew silently** – so you don't notice them until your card declines

- **Buy now, pay later** makes it feel like you got something for free *(spoiler: you didn't)*

You're not weak if you fall for this stuff. You're just human. They count on that.

Start asking:

- *"How are they making money off of me right now?"*

- *"Do I even remember signing up for this?"*

- *"Would I still buy this if I had to hand over actual cash?"*

Awareness is power. And you deserve to know when you're being played.

Step 4: Emergency Money is Not a Myth

If you can start putting aside anything, even $10 a week, do it. Why? Because flat tires, busted phones, and surprise medical bills are guaranteed to happen.

You don't need a huge savings account right away. Just a little space between you and disaster.

That space = peace.

A few tricks:

- Set up auto-transfer to savings, even a small one

- Use a separate bank for savings so you're not tempted to dip into it

- Name the account something annoying like "**DON'T TOUCH THIS**" if it helps

Bonus Tip: Budgeting is Self-Respect, Not Punishment

You're not "restricting" yourself when you manage your money. You're protecting your future self from stress and panic.

You deserve:

- To not overdraft

- To be able to buy groceries without sweating

- To say yes to things that matter because you said no to things that didn't

Budgeting isn't about saying no all the time.

It's about knowing when to say yes – and feeling good about it.

Quick Wins: Money Math That Makes Sense

- Look at your bank account once a week – even if you're scared

- Cancel one subscription you forgot you had

- Pick one thing to pause spending on this month *(e.g. fast food, apps, late-night impulse buys)*

- Try a "no spend day" once a week

- Start a savings stash – even if it's a literal jar labeled "future me"

You're not bad with money. You're just learning how to drive it instead of being dragged behind it.

You don't need to be rich. You just need to stop feeling like you're drowning.

And you can.

🎯 CHAPTER 5:
What the Hell Is a Credit Score?
(Or: The Secret Scoreboard That Decides If You Get a Car or Live in a Dumpster)

Nobody tells you what a credit score really is until it's already messed up. And by then, you're just hoping to get approved for a used couch and a sad apartment with a broken mailbox.

So here's the deal: your credit score is like a reputation number for your money behavior. You don't have to be rich to have good credit. You just have to prove that when someone lets you borrow money, you're going to pay it back – on time, every time.

Let's break it down in plain English.

Step 1: What Even Is a Credit Score?

It's a number between 300 and 850 that tells lenders how "risky" you are when it comes to paying bills or loans.

- Above 720 = great

- Around 650–720 = fine

- Below 600 = problems start showing up

This number affects:

- Whether you can get a credit card, car loan, apartment, or mortgage

- What interest rate you get (which can mean hundreds more or less paid over time)

- How "trustworthy" you look on paper

And you don't even have to do anything wrong to get a low score. You can just... not exist financially yet. Fun!

Step 2: What Makes a Credit Score Go Up or Down?

Here's what the mysterious credit gods care about:

1. **Do you pay your bills on time?**

    - Late = bad. On time = gold star.

2. **Do you owe a lot compared to your limit?**

    - Example: You have a $1,000 credit card limit and owe $950? Bad.

    - You owe $100 instead? Nice.

3. **Do you have any long-standing accounts?**

    - Older accounts = better credit history

4. **Do you apply for credit constantly?**

    - Too many applications = red flag

5. **Do you have different types of credit?**

    - Like a credit card and a car loan or student loan = good variety

You don't need to check every box – but the first two matter a lot.

✳ Step 3: How to Build Credit Without Ruining Your Life

If you're just starting out or trying to repair a mess, here's how to get on track:

- **Start with a secured credit card**

    - You put down a deposit, then borrow against it

    - Use it for small things (gas, groceries)

    - Pay it off in full every single month

- **Use less than 30% of your credit limit**

    - If your limit is $500, try not to carry more than $150 on it

- **Set up autopay if possible**

    - So you never miss a due date

- **Don't close your oldest accounts unless you have to**

    - The age of your credit history matters

- **Don't max out cards – even if you're desperate**

    - Credit scoring systems hate that

Step 4: Check Your Score and Reports (It's Free)

You're allowed to check your credit reports from the three big credit bureaus for free once a year:

- Experian
- Equifax
- TransUnion

Go to: **AnnualCreditReport.com**

That's the legit one.

Some credit card apps and banks also show your credit score. That's fine for checking your number, but **the full reports** help you spot errors or old debt that's dragging you down.

Step 5: If You Mess Up, Don't Hide – Call

This is where personal advocacy matters most.

If you made a mistake – missed a payment, got behind on a bill – **don't just ignore it. Pick up the phone.**

Credit card companies, landlords, lenders – they're not out to ruin your life. They just want their money. And if you call them and explain your situation:

- They'll often give you a one-time pass and not report the late payment

- They might offer a payment plan

- They'll usually work with you – especially if you're polite, honest, and proactive

This kind of communication can **literally protect your credit score** from a hit. It also builds confidence. Calling sucks, yes – but it saves you. And once you do it, the next time is easier.

So here's your life tip:

Be brave. Advocate for yourself. Call before it becomes a crisis.

🔍 Bonus Tip: You Can Recover From Bad Credit

Credit isn't a personality trait. It's a moving number. And it *can* go back up – even if you've made mistakes.

You don't have to be perfect. You just have to be **consistently okay** for a while:

- Keep your usage low
- Make small payments on time
- Don't disappear from the system

Credit is like trust – it builds slowly. But it *does* build.

📌 Quick Wins: Credit Score Survival Guide

- Set reminders for due dates – or use autopay
- Only charge what you can afford to pay off
- Use credit cards like tools, not like "free money"
- Check your credit reports once a year
- Call if you mess up – don't disappear

▓ Final Word:

You don't need to obsess over your credit score. You just need to respect it, because it can mess up your life if you ignore it – and make life easier when you don't.

And now? You're officially someone who understands credit better than most adults.

You win.

 **CHAPTER 6:**
Getting a Job (and Keeping It)
(Or: How to Convince People to Pay You Without Feeling Like a Fraud)

Jobs are weird. You need one to make money, but you also have to act like you're already a responsible, confident adult before anyone will hire you. It's a strange little performance that no one trains you for, and it can feel like you're just faking your way through it.

But here's the secret: *everyone is kind of faking it at first.* Confidence comes from *doing* – not waiting until you feel worthy.

This chapter is your shortcut to landing a job and keeping it, even if your résumé is short, your anxiety is loud, and your imposter syndrome is throwing shade in the background.

💼 Step 1: Figure Out What You Can Do (It's More Than You Think)

You don't need a degree or fancy job history to have valuable skills.

Ask yourself:

- Can I work with people?

- Can I stay calm under pressure?

- Am I reliable?

- Can I learn fast?

- Have I helped, built, solved, or organized anything before?

If you've ever:

- Taken care of kids

- Run a school club

- Fixed something

- Volunteered

- Tutored

- Helped a friend move

You've got transferable skills. You just need to name them clearly.

Step 2: Write a Resume That Doesn't Sound Like a Robot

Keep it simple. Keep it real.

- One page is fine

- Use bullet points

- Highlight things you've done, even outside of formal jobs

- Action words help: "managed," "organized," "created," "assisted," "solved"

Example bullet:

- Assisted customers and managed a busy front counter at local diner, balancing speed and friendliness in a fast-paced environment.

Translation: I can multitask, communicate, and not lose it under pressure.

Pro tip: You don't have to do this alone.

If you're not sure how to word your skills, let a tool like ChatGPT help. Seriously. It's free, and it's ridiculously good at turning real-life experience into professional bullet points.

Try saying:
"I helped run the school theater tech booth for two years and kept things organized. Can you help me write a resume bullet for that?"

Boom – instant translation.

Whether you've worked retail, babysat, volunteered, or just kept your friend group from falling apart during chaos, you've got skills. You just need help putting them into job-speak. *Ask for it. That's smart, not weak.*

🎤 Step 3: Don't Fear the Interview (It's a Conversation, Not a Trial)

You're not on trial. You're having a conversation to see if you're a good match.

Prep with these basics:

- Dress one notch nicer than you think you need to
- Practice answering common questions like:
  - "Tell me about yourself."
  - "What are your strengths?"
  - "Why do you want this job?"
- Have a question ready to ask them
  - ("What does a typical day here look like?" is a solid go-to)

If you're nervous, *say so.* It shows honesty and self-awareness.

And hey – *smile.* It does half the work.

Bonus mindset shift: Think of the interview like a first date.

- Both sides are trying to figure out if this will work

- You're allowed to ask questions

- You're allowed to walk away if something feels off

- And just like dating – *don't seem desperate*

Confidence isn't arrogance. It's knowing that your time and energy are worth something, too.

⊞ Step 4: Show Up, Speak Up, Follow Through

Once you've got the job, here's how to stand out:

- Show up on time (or early)
- Speak up if you're confused or need help
- Follow through on what you say you'll do

You don't need to be perfect. You just need to:

- Be reliable
- Be respectful
- Be willing to learn

That alone puts you ahead of most people.

📞 Step 5: If Something Goes Wrong, Don't Ghost – Communicate

Missed a shift? Made a mistake? *Don't vanish.*

- Call. Text. Show up and say something.

- Apologize if needed. Ask how to make it right.

- Most bosses care more about effort and accountability than perfection.

You *will* screw up sometimes. That's not failure. That's part of working.

How you handle it matters more than what went wrong.

🚀 Bonus Tip: You're Not Stuck Forever

This job? It's not your forever. It's just your next step.

Even if it's not your dream job, it might:

- Pay your bills

- Teach you new skills

- Connect you with better opportunities

- Give you confidence for the next thing

You're allowed to leave when something better comes along.
You're allowed to keep it if it's helping.
You're allowed to want more. *Always.*

 Quick Wins: Job-Hunting Confidence Boosters

- Ask someone you trust to look over your resume

- Practice a short "about me" speech so you're not frozen in interviews

- Apply even if you think you're not qualified – they'll train you

- Show up prepared and polite, and you're already ahead

- Remember: *you're not begging – you're offering your help in exchange for pay*

You don't need to know everything on day one.
You just need to show up, be honest, and try.

That's enough.
That's what keeps the paycheck coming.

CHAPTER 7:
Health Stuff You Can't Ignore Forever
(Or: Why "I'm Fine" Isn't a Health Plan)

You can go a surprisingly long time pretending you don't have a body. Skip checkups. Sleep like garbage. Eat mostly beige food. Ignore that weird pain in your side.

And then one day, everything catches up with you – and suddenly the system expects you to understand insurance, book appointments, and explain symptoms like you didn't just Google "why does my ankle feel crunchy."

This chapter is about the basics – taking care of yourself without getting overwhelmed or going broke. And yes, it's also about personal agency. Because speaking up for your health is one of the most grown-up, rebellious things you can do.

Step 1: The Bare Minimum Health Habits

You don't need to live at the gym or blend kale into your soul. You just need some basic routines that keep you functioning.

Start here:

- **Drink water**. You don't need to hit 8 glasses, but drink some water on purpose every day.

- **Sleep**. Most adults need 7–9 hours. If you can't get that, at least stop bragging about not sleeping. It's not cute.

- **Eat something with color**. A vegetable. A fruit. Anything that didn't come in a crinkly wrapper.

- **Move your body**. Not "exercise." Just move. Walk, stretch, dance, vacuum like a maniac – whatever works.

- **Listen to your body**. Pain, fatigue, anxiety – none of those are weakness. They're signals. Don't ignore them.

Step 2: Know the Doctors You Might Actually Need

You don't need a team of specialists, but you do need to know who handles what.

Here's a cheat sheet:

- **Primary care doctor (PCP):** Your go-to for checkups, meds, questions, and referrals

- **Urgent care:** For minor emergencies – burns, sprains, infections, "do I need stitches?" situations

- **Therapist or counselor:** Mental health support (and not just when you're in crisis)

- **Gynecologist:** For reproductive health (not just for women – trans folks, too)

- **Dentist:** Yes, you do need to go. Yes, they know if you floss.

- **Optometrist:** Eye health. Glasses. Headache prevention.

You don't have to go all at once. Start with one. Schedule it. Done.

Step 3: Insurance Isn't Magic – But It's Not Hopeless

Health insurance is confusing on purpose. But once you learn a few terms, it's less terrifying:

- **Premium:** What you pay monthly just to have insurance

- **Deductible:** What you have to pay before insurance kicks in

- **Copay:** A set fee you pay for a visit (like $20 at the doctor)

- **Out-of-pocket max:** The most you'll have to pay in a year before insurance covers everything

Pro tip: If you're under 26, you can probably stay on a parent's insurance.

If not, look at state programs, Medicaid, school insurance, or ACA plans at healthcare.gov.

It's not perfect. But some coverage is better than none – especially when you need it most.

Step 3.5: You Probably Have More Options Than You Think

Here's something nobody tells you: **most medical bills are negotiable.** And most people don't know how many programs exist to help you.

If you get a hospital bill and you can't afford it:

- **Call the billing department.** Say, "I can't pay this."

- They'll often ask what you *can* pay – and they'll accept $5/month just to keep it moving.

- That kind of payment plan usually doesn't go on your credit report. It's a handshake agreement, not a collection.

Also:

- **Most hospitals have charity care programs by** law

- **Nonprofits and community health centers** often offer sliding scale fees

- Urgent care is cheaper than the ER in almost every case

- You might qualify for Medicaid and not know it

- **Some providers will literally reduce your bill** if you just ask them to

The system is frustrating, yes. But it's not impossible.

You don't have to be rich. You just have to be persistent.
Start calling. Start asking. You'll be surprised what's available.

Step 4: Mental Health = Real Health

Anxiety, depression, burnout, ADHD, trauma – these aren't personality flaws. They're health conditions.

You are allowed to:

- Go to therapy

- Ask for medication

- Take a mental health day

- Admit that you're not okay – and still be strong as hell

If your brain is fighting you, you're not broken. You're a person who deserves support.

Hot tip: Community health clinics, campus resources, and apps like BetterHelp or Talkspace offer options if you can't afford private therapy.

📞 Step 5: Speak Up – You're the One Living in This Body

Doctors aren't gods. You don't have to be passive in your own care.

- Ask questions. Even if they seem dumb.

- Take notes if you're overwhelmed.

- If something feels wrong, say so.

- If they ignore you, get a second opinion.

You don't need to know everything – but you do get a say.

And yes, calling for appointments can be scary. Do it anyway. You're worth the discomfort. That phone call is a power move.

Bonus Tip: If You Can't Do Everything, Do Something

Health isn't all-or-nothing. Some days, winning looks like:

- Drinking a glass of water
- Making one phone call
- Taking one walk
- Saying "I don't feel okay today" out loud

Every one of those is a form of care. Every one counts.

Quick Wins: Health Survival Checklist

- Schedule one checkup this month (doctor, dentist, therapist – your choice)

- Add a reusable water bottle to your bag or desk

- Pick one "real food" item to eat every day (apple, carrot, not chips)

- Stretch for 2 minutes in the morning

- Make a list of health stuff you've been avoiding. Pick one thing. Do it.

You don't need to have it all together. You just need to start paying attention.
You don't need a six-pack or a therapist on retainer. You just need to not give up on yourself.

Your health matters. Because you matter.

▦ CHAPTER 8:
People Boundaries, Burnout, and Saying No
(Or: How to Stop Being Everything for Everyone Without Setting Your Life on Fire)

There comes a point in everyone's life when you realize that be-ing nice all the time doesn't feel good – it feels like slowly disap-pearing. You say yes when you mean no. You take on too much. You answer texts when you're exhausted. You keep the peace while your insides scream.

This chapter is about how to stop doing that.

Boundaries aren't walls. They're doors – with locks you control. You're allowed to open them. You're allowed to shut them. You're allowed to say, "Not today, thanks." And you're allowed to mean it.

Step 1: Understand What a Boundary Actually Is

A boundary is not being mean.
It's not rejection.
It's not controlling someone else.

A boundary is a line you draw around your time, energy, space, or feelings to protect your well-being. That's it.

- "I can't talk right now."

- "I'm not comfortable with that."

- "No, thank you."

- "Please don't speak to me that way."

Boundaries are how you teach people how to treat you.

⚠️ Step 2: Spot the Signs That You Need a Boundary

You might need a boundary if:

- You feel anxious when someone texts you

- You're constantly exhausted but still saying yes

- You feel resentful toward people you care about

- You say "it's fine" when it's very much not fine

- You haven't had alone time in forever but feel guilty asking for it

If you feel like you're falling apart but can't stop showing up anyway?

That's burnout. And it's your body begging for boundaries.

Step 3: Saying "No" Without Guilt (or Less of It, Anyway)

"No" is a complete sentence – but you can dress it up if you need to.

Here are some options:

- "I can't take that on right now."
- "That's not going to work for me."
- "I'd love to help, but I'm overcommitted."
- "Thanks for thinking of me, but I'll pass."
- "Not this time."

You don't owe a full explanation. You don't have to justify your needs.

You're not selfish. You're a person with limits – and protecting those limits keeps you from breaking.

Step 4: What Happens If People Get Mad?

Sometimes, when you set a boundary, people won't like it.

That doesn't mean you're wrong. It just means they were benefiting from you having none.

Let them be uncomfortable. That's theirs to sit with – not yours to fix.

- You are not responsible for other people's feelings.

- You are not required to be available all the time.

- You are not the emotional sponge for your friend group, family, or job.

Let go of the myth that kindness means self-abandonment. Real kindness includes you, too.

Step 5: Energy Is Currency – Spend It Wisely

Your time is valuable. Your energy is finite. Every time you say yes to one thing, you're saying no to something else.

Ask yourself:

- Do I want to do this, or do I feel obligated?

- Am I saying yes to avoid guilt – or because it genuinely feels right?

- If I say yes now, what will I have to say no to later?

Protect your peace like it's your rent money. Because when it runs out, everything gets unstable.

The Balance of Boundaries

Boundaries are about care – not control.

A healthy boundary protects your peace while still considering the people you care about. It says:

> *"I want to stay in this relationship, and this is how I can do that without burning out."*

But some people swing too hard the other way. They use boundaries to:

- Avoid difficult conversations

- Shut people down instead of listening

- Justify selfishness

- Push people away while pretending they're being "healthy"

That's not a boundary. That's a wall.

You don't need to be a doormat – but you also don't need to be a bulldozer. The goal is balance:

- Speak your needs clearly

- Listen to the other person's, too

- Set limits – but be kind about it

- Protect your energy *without cutting everyone out*

Boundaries help relationships survive long-term – when they're built with honesty and empathy.

Bonus Tip: Boundaries Are a Skill, Not a Personality Trait

If you struggle with this, you're not broken. You're probably just used to putting others first because you were taught that was "good."

But boundaries are learned.

You can practice. You can improve. You can screw it up, try again, and get better.

Start small. Practice with easy things. Build your boundary muscles over time.

Every "no" you say to something that drains you is a "yes" to something that sustains you.

Quick Wins: Boundary Practice Guide

- Say no to one small thing this week – and don't explain yourself

- Delay a reply when you feel pressured to say yes

- Block out one hour this week just for yourself – non-negotiable

- Write a list of people or situations that drain you, then brainstorm boundaries for each

- Remind yourself: You're allowed to disappoint people. You are not required to be endlessly agreeable

Your time matters. Your energy matters. *You* matter.
And you are allowed – *completely, unapologetically allowed* – to say no, protect your peace, and stop lighting yourself on fire to keep other people warm.

CHAPTER 9:

Mistakes, Meltdowns, and Moving On
(Or: You're Allowed to Screw Up and Still Succeed)

Here's the truth no one puts on motivational posters:

You're going to mess up.

You'll forget something. Drop the ball. Snap at someone. Miss a deadline. Hit a wall.

You might even melt down in a bathroom stall, then walk out and pretend everything's fine.

This chapter is about what happens *after* that.

Because screwing up isn't the end. It's part of learning. And if you can push through the shame and self-doubt, you'll find something way more powerful than perfection: **resilience**.

🔍 Step 1: Separate Mistakes from Identity

You made a mistake. You are not a mistake.

You failed a test. You're not a failure.
You forgot to show up. That doesn't mean you're irresponsible forever.

Messing up is part of being human. It means you're trying. It means you care. And it means you're still learning.

Don't turn one bad moment into a lifelong label. You're more than that.

Step 2: Own It (Gently, Not Dramatically)

If you mess up, say so. That's it.

- "I missed the deadline – I'm sorry."

- "That was my mistake. What can I do to fix it?"

- "I didn't handle that well. I'll do better next time."

You don't need to grovel. You don't need to disappear. You just need to own it, fix what you can, and move forward.

Accountability builds trust faster than pretending you didn't mess up in the first place.

Step 3: Learn the Pattern, Not Just the Lesson

Ask yourself:

- What made that mistake happen?

- Was I tired, rushed, afraid to say no, disorganized, or distracted?

- Can I put something in place to prevent this next time?

Every mistake holds a clue about your systems, habits, and triggers.

Dig into that. That's how you grow.

Step 4: Let Yourself Feel It – Then Move

It's okay to feel embarrassed, frustrated, or overwhelmed. Cry if you need to. Take a walk. Text someone who gets it.
But don't sit in that shame spiral forever.

Feel it. Process it. And then do something small to move forward. Send the email. Wash the dish. Make the call. Write the apology.

Movement breaks the spiral. Momentum brings confidence back.

💼 Step 5: Resilience Isn't Bouncing Back – It's Rebuilding Smarter

You don't have to "bounce back" like nothing happened. That's not the goal.

Resilience is when you fall, pause, swear a little, figure out what went wrong, and build something better out of it.

It's grit. It's grace. It's messy as hell. But it's also strength.

You've made it through 100% of your bad days so far.
You're more capable than you think.

💡 Bonus Tip: You're Not the Only One Struggling

Everyone you admire has failed, broken down, quit something too soon, or stayed too long in the wrong place.

Everyone is winging it at least a little.

You're not falling behind. You're just in progress.

 Quick Wins: Mistake Recovery Kit

- Take a breath. Literally. Stop and breathe.

- Say "I messed up" – out loud. It's powerful.

- Make a tiny fix, even if you can't fix the whole thing

- Talk to someone who reminds you of who you are – not just what you did

- Ask yourself: *"What would I say to a friend who did this?"* Then say it to yourself

Screwing up isn't the end. It's just a page in the middle of your story.

You don't need to be perfect. You just need to keep going.

Because you're worth the effort – even on the messy days.

◉ CHAPTER 10:
Why People Judge You Instantly
(Or: How to Look Like You Belong Even When You Feel Like a Total Imposter)

We all want to be judged by what's inside—our intelligence, our values, our sparkling personality hidden under three layers of social awkwardness.

But here's the reality: People judge you in seconds.

Before you speak. Before you show how brilliant you are. Before you explain that your hoodie is ironic.

And that doesn't make people shallow. It makes them human.

This chapter isn't about faking who you are. It's about understanding the signals you're sending—and learning how to control them on purpose, so the outside matches the capable person you already are on the inside.

Step 1: People Notice What You Wear—Even If They Shouldn't

You don't have to be trendy. You don't have to be a fashion expert.

You just have to look like you made an effort to exist in the same dimension as everyone else.

Why it matters:

- People use clothing as a shortcut to guess if you're responsible, approachable, or prepared.

- If you're wildly overdressed or underdressed, it can distract from what you're saying.

- Clothes signal whether you understand the environment you're stepping into.

This isn't about changing who you are. It's about making sure people see you clearly—not get hung up on your anime hoodie or pajama pants.

If you're not sure what to wear, look around. See what others in that space are wearing, and aim to match the energy—not copy it, but respect it.

🗣️ Step 2: Your Face, Voice, and Body Are All Talking—Even If You're Silent

This is where a lot of people get misunderstood.

You might feel fine but look angry.
You might be nervous and come off as cold.
You might be so focused on what to say that you forget your body's saying something already.

Common nonverbal things people misread:

- No eye contact = disinterested or untrustworthy

- Low voice = uncertain or unfriendly

- Slouched posture = low energy or low confidence

- Fidgeting or pacing = anxious or distracted

- Blank or neutral expression = upset or bored

You don't have to turn into a motivational speaker.
You just need to check in with your face and body from time to time.

Are you scowling without realizing it? Slumped over? Whispering your sentences into your sweater?

These things can be adjusted—gently, without changing who you are.

Start by practicing in the mirror or recording yourself. See what others see. Adjust what feels right.

🎯 Step 3: It's Not Fake to Make an Effort

Some people worry that changing how they dress or hold them-selves is dishonest. But let's flip that:

• You're not changing your personality.

• You're not pretending to be extroverted.

• You're just learning the rules of the room so you can be seen clearly and treated fairly.

Think of it like learning how to write a good email. You still write your thoughts—just in a way that people will understand and respect.

This is no different.

Quick Wins: First Impressions Without the Panic

- Look in the mirror before you leave. Check your face, clothes, posture. Reset if needed.

- Make eye contact for a second or two when you greet someone. That's enough.

- Practice introducing yourself out loud—just once—before you walk in.

- Dress one notch nicer than you think you need to. It shows you care.

- Smile. Just a little one. People notice.

You don't need to be perfect. You just need to be aware.

First impressions matter—but they're not about pretending.

They're about showing up in a way that helps others see the real you.

And the real you? Is worth being seen.

CHAPTER 11:
Dressing Like You Belong
(Without Feeling Like a
Corporate Clone)
(Or: Clothes Shouldn't Cost You Credibility—
Or Your Personality)

Let's get this out of the way: you don't need to "conform" to be successful. But like it or not, your clothes are talking before you are. And depending on what they're saying, people may make assumptions that have nothing to do with your actual skills or potential.

This isn't about selling out. It's about knowing how to visually say, "I get it. I belong here."

You can still be yourself—you're just adjusting the volume.

🧠 Step 1: People Read Clothes Like a Code (Even If It's Unfair)

Clothes tell a story before you speak. People might assume:

- You're reliable or messy

- Confident or checked-out

- Professional or still mentally at home in bed

They won't always get it right, but it happens fast. You can choose to fight that... or learn how to speak the visual language just enough to get past the bouncer at the door.

This isn't about erasing your personality. It's about removing distractions so people focus on you, not your outfit.

📷 Step 2: Learn the Vibe of the Room

Start by decoding what "fitting in" actually looks like in the environment you're walking into.

- Corporate job? Think solid colors, button-ups, fitted slacks, simple shoes.

- Creative workplace? Think polished-casual—neat jeans, nice sneakers, cool accessories.

- Trades or field work? Practical, clean, and functional—bonus points for weatherproof layers and sturdy boots.

- Remote or hybrid? Business on top, comfort on the bottom (just don't forget which half the webcam sees).

Look around. What are others wearing in the space you want to be part of? You don't have to match perfectly—just aim to be in the same general zone.

💼 Step 3: Clothes That Work and Feel Like You

You don't need a huge wardrobe. Just a few key pieces that signal you made an effort:

- A decent pair of pants that fit you well

- A plain, clean button-down or blouse

- A pair of shoes that aren't falling apart

- A jacket or sweater that looks intentional

A note on comfort: If clothes feel like a costume, you're going to act like you're pretending. Find things that are appropriate and let you breathe. Stretchy fabrics. Comfortable shoes. Things that make you feel like you, just turned up a notch.

And if you're on a tight budget? Thrift stores, discount outlets, and online deals are your best friends. No one needs to know where it came from. They'll just see that you showed up ready.

Step 4: Hygiene and Grooming = Invisible Credibility

This part isn't glamorous, but it matters.

You don't need salon treatments or designer products. You just need:

- Clean hair

- Clean clothes

- Clean nails

- Basic deodorant

- Breath that won't send someone into fight-or-flight

This stuff doesn't usually get compliments—but when it's missing, people notice. Showing up fresh, tidy, and put-together says, "I respect myself and this space." That message? Super powerful.

Step 5: Style Isn't the Enemy of Authenticity

You can still wear color. You can still accessorize. You can still bring your culture, identity, or neurodivergent comfort needs into how you dress.

The goal isn't to become bland. The goal is to understand when and how to turn the dial up or down depending on where you are.

You're not faking it. You're choosing the version of you that fits this moment—and that's power.

🧺 Quick Wins: Dressing Without the Stress

- Pick one outfit you feel great in and upgrade it slightly (nicer shoes, ironed shirt, a jacket)

- Try on your "interview clothes" and make sure they still fit and feel okay

- Donate anything that makes you feel weird, itchy, or 200% not you

- Build one basic, go-to "I have to look normal" outfit you can grab in a panic

- Wash your go-to clothes regularly. Clean beats expensive every time

You don't have to be fancy. You don't have to be trendy.
You just have to show that you get the message—and that you belong in the room.

You've got something to offer. Let your clothes support that, not compete with it.

CHAPTER 12:
Body Language—
The Silent Killer
of Career Growth
(Or: How to Look Like You Belong Before You Even Speak)

People listen with their eyes.

Before they hear a word you say, they've already picked up on your posture, your energy, your "vibe." And fair or not, those first impressions can open doors—or quietly close them.

You don't need to become a walking TED Talk. But a few body language adjustments can help people see you the way you want to be seen: capable, calm, and someone worth listening to.

💪 Step 1: Posture Isn't About Perfection—It's About Presence

You don't have to stand like a soldier. But you do want to look like you're present—not shrinking into the background or trying to become one with your chair.

Try this:

- Sit or stand with your shoulders back (not rigid, just open)

- Keep your chin level—not down like you're apologizing, or up like you're judging

- Take up a little space. You're allowed to exist here.

Even if you don't feel confident yet, this kind of posture signals confidence—and helps you start to feel it.

🧘 Step 2: Fidgeting, Twitching, and Nervous Energy—What to Do Instead

We all have nervous habits. Pen-clicking. Knee-bouncing. Hair-twirling. Looking like you're fighting invisible bees.

These things aren't bad—but they can distract from what you're saying, especially in interviews or meetings.

Instead, try grounding habits:

- Keep your hands loosely folded on the table

- Plant your feet on the floor

- Hold something small if you need to (a pen, a paperclip, a ring)

- Pause and breathe when you feel the urge to scramble

You don't have to be perfectly still. You just want to look like your brain and body are in the same place.

Step 3: Personal Space Is a Real Thing (And Yes, It Varies)

Some people grew up in cultures or families where close contact is normal. Others get anxious if someone stands within arm's reach.

Here's a safe default for work and formal settings: an arm's length of space.

Close enough to engage, far enough to breathe.

If someone steps back, don't take it personally. They're just resetting their comfort zone. You're not doing anything wrong.

😶 Step 4: Your Face Might Be Sending Mixed Messages

Some of us were born with resting blank face. Or resting tired face. Or, let's be honest—resting "I hate everything" face.

This doesn't mean you're scary. It just means people might misunderstand you.

What helps:

- A soft smile—not a big one, just a little lift

- Making eye contact for a second or two when you greet someone

- Nodding when others speak (it shows you're listening)

- Keeping your eyebrows from full "judgment mode" (unless that's what you meant)

These are gentle signals that say: "I'm present, I'm safe, and I'm tuned in."

🎯 Step 5: You Can Practice This Without Feeling Fake

This part trips people up. It's easy to think:

"I don't want to be fake. I want to just be myself."

But think of it like learning any other tool. You're not faking who you are.

You're just getting better at expressing what's already true about you.

You care. You want to do well. You want to be understood.

Practicing body language that supports that message isn't fake—it's smart.

It helps the world see what's great about you sooner.

🛠 Quick Wins: Body Language Tune-Ups

- Record yourself talking for one minute and notice your posture, face, and gestures

- Try a two-minute posture reset: stand tall, breathe deep, drop your shoulders

- Practice a calm entrance—walk into a room slowly, smile gently, look around

- Watch a confident speaker and mirror their posture (don't mimic—just notice)

- Ask someone you trust, "How do I come across in a room?" and really listen

You don't need to turn into a robot. You just need to understand the signals you're sending—and learn how to align them with who you really are.

Because you're someone worth seeing clearly. And this helps make that happen.

💬 CHAPTER 13:
The Art of Small Talk (Even If You Hate It)
(Or: How to Speak Human Without Setting Off the Awkward Alarm)

Let's be honest: small talk feels fake.
It's surface-level, repetitive, and often sounds like people are reading off a script they didn't know they memorized.

But here's the thing—small talk is the doorway.
It's how people test the waters. It's the warm-up before the deeper conversation. And if you skip it entirely, people might feel like you're slamming the door before they even get to know you.

The goal isn't to become a chatterbox. The goal is to get through it smoothly so people feel safe talking to you—and so you can get to the good stuff faster.

🪨 Step 1: Why Small Talk Exists (It's Not Just Noise)

Small talk is like stretching before exercise.
It's not the main event—but it prevents things from pulling, snapping, or falling apart unexpectedly.

People use it to:

- Check your mood

- Ease into conversation

- Signal friendliness

- Build trust in low-stakes moments

It's not about the words. It's about the vibe. When you get that, the pressure drops.

🧠 Step 2: Easy Scripts for When You Freeze Up

You don't need a library of topics. You just need a few fallback lines that work in almost any setting.

3 foolproof openers:

- "Hey, how's your day going so far?"

- "Busy today, or kind of slow?"

- "Is this your first time here / working on this / dealing with this madness?"

3 safe follow-ups:

- "That makes sense."

- "I totally get that."

- "Yeah, I've heard it's been like that lately."

Bonus: Just repeating the last thing they said with a question tone often works.

Them: "Traffic was terrible."

You: "Traffic?"

(They'll keep talking. You're in.)

🚫 Step 3: Topics to Avoid Unless You Know the Person Well

- Politics

- Religion

- Intense personal stories

- Medical stuff

- Your darkest existential thoughts

- Anything that makes someone go "Whoa... okay then"

When in doubt: keep it light. Keep it shared. Keep it brief.

Think weather, weekend plans, shows, pets, food, or "this weird day."

Step 4: The Exit Strategy (Leave Gracefully, Not Abruptly)

Sometimes you need to bounce. Social battery = drained. Here's how to leave without sounding rude or panicked:

- "Well, I should let you get back to it—good talking to you."

- "I'm going to grab some water / find a seat / check my messages. Nice meeting you!"

- "I need to sneak out for a second—hope the rest of your day's easy."

People appreciate the heads-up. And you'll feel better walking away on your own terms.

✿ Step 5: You're Not Weird for Disliking Small Talk

So many people hate it. You're not alone.

But getting a little better at it? It opens doors. It helps people see that you're open, safe, and approachable—even if you're not a social butterfly.

Think of small talk like turning a doorknob.

You don't have to love the doorknob. You just have to twist it to get to the room where the real conversation happens.

🎯 Quick Wins: Small Talk Without the Dread

- Practice 3 go-to lines in the mirror or out loud in the car

- Ask one "safe" question at your next work event, meeting, or elevator ride

- If you freeze, just smile and say, "I'm still waking up to-day—how's your morning?"

- Watch someone else do small talk well and borrow their phrasing

- Remember: You're not being judged for being quiet—you're being appreciated for making the effort

Small talk isn't about being extroverted.
It's about creating just enough connection to be seen—and to make others feel seen, too.

You don't have to love it. But you can get good at it. And that's enough.

✉ CHAPTER 14:
Email & Messaging—
How Not to Sound
Like a Weirdo
(Or: How to Write Like a Functional Human Without Overthinking Every Exclamation Point)

Writing to people at work can be weirdly terrifying.

You stare at the screen for ten minutes trying to decide if "Hi" sounds too casual or if "Hello" makes you sound like an alien. You reread the message twelve times and still wonder if you're about to get fired for how you signed off.

It doesn't have to be that intense.

This chapter is here to help you write emails and messages that sound like you—polite, clear, and confident—without spiraling into overthinking.

⚛ Step 1: The Goal Is Clarity, Not Perfection

You don't need to sound fancy. You don't need to use corporate buzzwords or speak like a 19th-century butler.

You just need to be:

- Clear about what you're asking

- Respectful in your tone

- Professional enough to be taken seriously

That's it. If the person reading your message understands what you want and doesn't think you're yelling or panicking, you win.

Step 2: How to Open Like a Normal Person

You don't have to reinvent the greeting every time. Here are safe, flexible openers that work in 99% of work situations:

- "Hi [Name],"

- "Good morning," / "Good afternoon,"

- "Hey [Name]," (okay for people you're familiar with)

Avoid: "To whom it may concern," unless you're writing to a ghost.

You don't need a huge opener. Just something that says, "I'm speaking to you like a fellow adult."

📝 Step 3: Keep the Message Short and Focused

Most people skim. They don't want to read a novel.

Try this structure:

1. Greeting

2. Why you're writing

3. What you need or want to say

4. A polite sign-off

Example:

Hi Jordan,

Just wanted to follow up on the project timeline.
Do you have an update on when the final piece will be ready?

Thanks so much,

Jen

Short. Clear. Polite. You don't need to add a life story or a disclaimer about how anxious you feel. They'll get it.

📣 Step 4: Emojis, Exclamations, and Tone—Where's the Line?

You want to sound friendly—but not like you're yelling through a smile.

Use exclamation points sparingly. One is fine. Two = enthusiastic. Three = you've officially left the building.

Emojis? In formal emails, skip them. In chats or DMs with coworkers, a smiley or thumbs-up is fine—if the vibe already feels relaxed.

Too much:

Hi!! Just checking in!!! 😂 💀 🔥 LOL I'm dying over here!!! 😅 🤪 🚨 —[Person you're now worried about]

Better:

Hey—just wanted to check in. Any updates on the plan? Thanks!

Calm. Human. Professional. That's the sweet spot.

🪓 Step 5: Signing Off Without Stressing Out

Choose a sign-off that fits the tone and relationship.

Formal:

- Best regards
- Sincerely
- Thank you

Friendly/neutral:

- Best
- Thanks
- Talk soon

Casual:

- Take care
- All the best
- Cheers (only if you're British or feeling bold)

You don't have to be clever. You just need to close the message like someone who's not panicking.

✦ Quick Wins: Writing Without the Spiral

- Use a simple email template and reuse it when you're stuck

- Read your message out loud—does it sound calm and clear? Good.

- If you're unsure, ask: "Would I be confused if I got this message?"

- Save one or two sign-offs and stick with them

- Trust that tone comes from your words—not your emoji count

You don't have to be the world's smoothest communicator. You just have to write like someone who respects the reader and knows what they're asking for.

You're not weird. You're learning the rhythm. And you're doing great.

CHAPTER 15:

Meetings & Conversations—How to Speak Up Without Overthinking It
(Or: How to Say Something Without Your Brain Screaming "Abort Mission!")

Some people love to talk. They raise their hand. They speak up in meetings. They confidently jump into conversations and somehow don't die from embarrassment afterward.

For the rest of us? Speaking up can feel like jumping off a cliff— every word gets rerouted through panic, doubt, and a ten-second internal debate about whether or not we're about to sound dumb.

This chapter is for that rest-of-us crowd.

You don't need to become a non-stop talker. You just need to know how to speak up clearly and calmly when it matters—and how to stop spiraling about it afterward.

🧠 Step 1: Prep a Few Go-To Phrases Ahead of Time

If you freeze when it's your turn to speak, don't wait for brilliance to strike. Instead, have a few lines ready to go—phrases that buy you time or ease you into the moment.

Examples:

- "I have a quick thought on that..."

- "Can I add something from a slightly different angle?"

- "This might be small, but I think it could help..."

These phrases signal, "Hey, I'm participating," without making you feel like you need to deliver a TED Talk.

You don't have to be profound. You just have to be present.

Step 2: Slower = Smarter (Yes, Really)

Most people rush when they're nervous. Their voice speeds up, their sentences tangle, and their brain tries to eject mid-sentence.

Try this instead:

- Take one breath before speaking

- Talk slower than you think you need to

- Pause between thoughts—even a half-second helps

Slowing down makes you sound more confident, more thoughtful, and way easier to follow. It also gives your brain time to catch up with your mouth.

⧗ Step 3: Don't Wait for the "Perfect Moment"

Sometimes you hesitate too long and the conversation moves on. That's okay—it happens to everyone. But if you're always waiting for a flawless opening, you'll miss every chance.

Instead:

- Look for a natural pause

- Raise your hand if it's a meeting

- Use a soft interruption: "Just to jump in real quick..." or "Sorry, can I add one thing?"

People actually appreciate when someone brings a new angle or gently circles back. You're not annoying—you're engaged.

🤝 Step 4: If You Disagree, Be Respectful (and Still Say It)

Disagreeing isn't rude. It's often useful. The key is how you do it.

Try:

- "I see what you're saying—I wonder if there's another way to look at it..."

- "I had a slightly different takeaway—can I share it?"

- "Here's a concern I had, just in case it helps shape the next steps..."

This kind of framing makes it safe for people to hear what you're saying. You're not attacking—you're contributing.

◉ Step 5: It's Okay to Rewind or Clarify

Ever say something and immediately wish you could redo it? Same.

Here's a secret: You're allowed to clean it up.
Just say:

- "Let me rephrase that real quick..."

- "I didn't explain that clearly—what I meant was..."

- "Sorry, let me back up a second..."

Nobody thinks less of you for correcting yourself. Honestly, it makes you look thoughtful and self-aware.

Quick Wins: Speaking Up Without Melting Down

- Pick one sentence you can say in the next meeting, even if it's simple

- Record yourself saying your intro or opinion—then listen back and tweak

- Practice pausing mid-sentence (it feels weird but sounds great)

- When you speak, focus on connection, not performance

- Afterward, give yourself credit—even if you only said one thing. You did it.

CHAPTER 16:
Navigating Office Politics When You'd Rather Not
(Or: How to Avoid Drama Without Getting Left Behind)

You don't have to like office politics.

You don't even have to play them hard.

But if you completely ignore them, people might pass you over—not because you aren't good at your job, but because they don't see you.

This chapter is about showing up in the workplace in a way that keeps your reputation solid, your relationships healthy, and your sanity intact—even if you'd rather just do your job and go home.

Step 1: "Just Doing My Job" Isn't Always Enough

You might think, "I'll just work hard and let that speak for itself."

That's noble. It's also not how most workplaces operate.

People don't just notice effort—they notice:

- Who speaks up

- Who's helpful

- Who's visible during meetings or projects

- Who gets along with the team

You don't need to be loud or political. But you do need to be seen.
Don't let your hard work stay hidden in the background.

👥 Step 2: Build Quiet Relationships (a.k.a. Strategic Friendliness)

You don't need to become besties with your coworkers. But you do need some baseline social glue.

Try this:

- Say hello when you arrive

- Ask someone how their day's going

- Join a group chat or lunch once in a while

- Send a quick "Nice work on that project" message

Small things matter. They create connection. They make you a person—not just a name on the staff list.

And when you do need help or support? Those quiet relationships will matter.

🦹 Step 3: Don't Trash Talk (Even When It's Fun)

Venting is tempting—especially if someone else is annoying, unfair, or clearly not pulling their weight.
But gossiping can boomerang fast—and it usually doesn't land on the person who deserved it.

If you need to vent:

- Do it outside work, with someone you trust

- Never put it in writing

- Avoid dragging people down just to bond with others

Your future self will thank you. So will your reputation.

◎ Step 4: Know What Your Boss Cares About (Even If It's Not What You Do)

You might be focused on task quality. Your boss might be focused on deadlines. Or client feedback. Or budget numbers.

Learn what your manager actually values, then make sure your work reflects that.

This isn't sucking up—it's aligning. It says, "I get what's important here, and I'm on board."

If you're not sure what they care about? Ask:

- "What's the top priority for you this week?"

- "What's something I can take off your plate?"

- "Anything I should shift focus toward?"

Simple questions. Big impact.

▪️ Step 5: Advocate for Yourself Without Apologizing

If you want a raise, a promotion, or a new project—ask for it. Don't wait to be "noticed." Sometimes people don't notice until you speak up.

Try:

- "I'd love to take on more responsibility—what would that look like?"

- "Could we check in about growth opportunities sometime soon?"

- "I'm proud of what I've done so far—can we talk about next steps?"

It's not selfish. It's how people move forward.

And if it helps: write your message out first. Rehearse it. You're not being pushy—you're being professional.

Quick Wins: Office Politics Without Losing Yourself

- Compliment one coworker this week for something they did well

- Ask a question in your next meeting—even if it's small

- Say one helpful thing to your boss that shows you're paying attention

- Join one workplace group chat or team lunch

- Choose not to participate in one gossip spiral and walk away clean

You don't need to scheme. You don't need to pretend.

But understanding how people connect and how reputations are built?

That's what keeps your talent from going unnoticed.

And you deserve to be seen.

CHAPTER 17:

Networking Without Wanting to Die
(Or: How to Talk to Strangers Without Sponta-
neous Combustion)

Networking sounds like a nightmare: a room full of people pretending they're not all uncomfortable, shaking hands, exchanging buzzwords, and pretending to love LinkedIn.

But here's the truth: networking doesn't have to be fake or exhausting. It's not about becoming the loudest person in the room—it's about building tiny bridges with people who might one day help you, work with you, or introduce you to someone who will.

This chapter will help you survive—and maybe even enjoy—networking, no matter how introverted, awkward, or "I'd rather be home" you feel.

Step 1: Redefine What Networking Actually Is

Networking isn't about:

- Passing out business cards like candy

- Collecting followers or contacts

- Impressing strangers with how cool you are

It is about:

- Making human connections

- Being curious about other people

- Planting seeds for future conversations

You're not here to close a deal. You're here to talk like a real person and maybe walk away with a useful contact—or just one good conversation.

That counts.

Step 2: Start With a Friendly One-Liner

Don't overthink your opener. People aren't expecting brilliance—they're just hoping you're not weird or aggressive.

Safe openers:

- "Hi, I'm [Your Name]. What brings you here?"

- "Hey—do you know many people at this event?"

- "So what kind of work do you do?"

- "Did you catch the speaker? What did you think?"

If you're in line for snacks or drinks:

- "They always say to network, but I'm mostly here for the free food."

Boom—relatable. You're in.

🎙 Step 3: Keep the Conversation Balanced

Networking isn't a monologue. Let the other person talk. Be curious.

Try:

- "How did you get into that?"

- "What do you enjoy most about it?"

- "Is that something you always wanted to do?"

You don't have to fake interest. Just look for common ground. If the conversation feels forced, it's okay to politely move on.

And if you accidentally interrupt or lose your train of thought? Smile and say:

- "Sorry, totally lost my thread. What were you saying?"

People appreciate realness.

Step 4: Know How to Leave the Conversation Gracefully

Not every interaction is meant to last forever. If the energy dies or the convo hits a wall, don't panic—just exit kindly.

Try:

- "It was really nice talking with you—I'm going to grab a drink and make the rounds, but I hope we cross paths again."

- "I want to make sure I meet a few more folks, but I really enjoyed this chat—mind if I find you on LinkedIn?"

- "Thanks for the conversation—hope the rest of the event goes well!"

You don't have to ghost. Just step out gently.

✉ Step 5: Follow Up Without Feeling Weird

If you meet someone and want to keep in touch, send a message within a day or two. Doesn't need to be fancy.

Example:

Hi [Name],

It was great chatting with you at [event]! I really appreciated hearing about [something specific].

Hope we can stay in touch.

-[You]

Simple. Professional. Friendly.

Even just one or two of these a year can lead to surprising opportunities later.

Quick Wins: Networking Without the Dread

- Make it your goal to talk to one person, not ten

- Bring a friend to events and split up halfway through

- Practice three safe openers so you don't freeze

- Carry a notebook or put notes in your phone so you remember who you met

- Follow up once—then let it go. No chasing needed.

Networking isn't about being charming.
It's about being present, polite, and human.

You already know how to do that. Just take a breath, say hi, and see what happens.

CHAPTER 18:
Taking Criticism Without Shutting Down or Fighting Back
(Or: How to Hear Feedback Without Melting Into a Puddle or Going Full Defense Mode)

Feedback is weird.

Someone tells you what you did "wrong" or "could improve," and even when it's kind and helpful, your brain might react like they just threw a chair at you.

You're not broken for feeling that way. Most of us were never taught how to take criticism well—it's emotional. It feels personal. And sometimes it is delivered poorly.

But learning how to handle feedback with calm, clarity, and confidence?

That's a power move.

⏸ Step 1: Pause Before You React

When someone gives you feedback—good, bad, or confusing—your first job is not to react.

Take a second. Breathe. Nod. Let your body catch up to your brain.

You don't have to agree or defend yourself right away. You just need to create space so you don't snap, shut down, or explode.

Try:

- "Thanks for the feedback—can I take a minute to think about it?"

- "Got it—I'll take a look at that and see what I can do."

- "That's helpful. I didn't see it that way."

Neutral. Calm. You're in control.

🔍 Step 2: Look for the Useful Parts—Not Just the Sting

Not all feedback is delivered well. Some of it's vague. Some is rude. Some comes from people who don't even fully get what you're doing.

But that doesn't mean there's nothing useful in it.

Ask yourself:

- What part of this might actually help me improve?

- Is there a specific point I can act on?

- Even if I don't like the tone—was the content valid?

You don't have to take all criticism. Just the pieces that help you get better.

💜 Step 3: Separate Your Work From Your Worth

This is huge: You are not your mistake.

Getting told "You missed a step" or "This needs improvement" is not the same as being told "You're bad at everything." But our brains can blur the line—especially if we already feel insecure.

Here's the truth: Smart, talented, amazing people get critiqued all the time.

It's not a sign you don't belong. It's a sign you're still learning—and willing to grow.

Take the note. Don't take the shame.

？ Step 4: Ask Questions If You're Not Sure What They Meant

Vague feedback is frustrating. "Can you tighten this up?" or "Just make it better" leaves you guessing.

You're allowed to ask:

- "Can you show me an example of what you're looking for?"

- "Is there a specific part that needs the most work?"

- "What would success look like here?"

Asking questions isn't pushback. It's clarity. And it shows you're serious about improving.

Step 5: Use Feedback to Level Up—Not Shut Down

Great feedback can help you:

- Learn faster

- Build trust with your team

- Avoid repeating mistakes

- Get promoted (seriously)

Even mediocre feedback can still help you learn to listen, stay cool, and respond professionally—which matters just as much.

You're not aiming for perfection. You're building resilience. That's the real win.

Quick Wins: Handling Criticism Like a Pro (Even If You're Panicking)

- Take a breath before responding—even a few seconds helps

- Repeat the feedback in your head as if it were said to a friend, not to you

- Ask one clarifying question before jumping to conclusions

- Write it down, walk away, and revisit it later with a calm brain

- Say "thank you" (even if your inner voice is yelling)—then decide what to keep or toss

Criticism isn't a personal attack. It's a tool.

And when you learn how to hold it without flinching, you become the sharpest thing in the room.

💼 CHAPTER 19:
Soft Skills That Actually Matter for Promotions
(Or: How to Get Noticed Without Sucking Up or Burning Out)

When people think about getting promoted, they picture someone who's really good at their job.

And yeah—that matters.

But a lot of promotions don't go to the person with the best technical skills.
They go to the person who's organized, communicates well, shows up reliably, and doesn't make other people's lives harder.

That's soft skills. That's what this chapter is about.

🕐 Step 1: Show Up When You Say You Will (It's Wildly Underrated)

Being reliable isn't glamorous—but it's powerful.

- Show up on time

- Meet your deadlines

- Communicate if you can't

- Don't ghost projects or meetings

- Let people know what to expect and when

This doesn't make you a suck-up. It makes you the person people trust—and that's the kind of person who gets promoted.

📫 Step 2: Respond to Messages Like a Grown-Up

You don't have to be glued to your inbox. But if someone emails or messages you about work, respond within a reasonable time—even just to say, "Got it. I'll follow up soon."

Silence creates stress.

A simple, short reply creates trust.

The people who move up are the ones who make communication easier, not harder.

Step 3: Stay Cool Under Pressure (Even If You're Internally Screaming)

No one's asking you to be a robot. But if you can stay calm when things go sideways—even just on the outside—people will start seeing you as leadership material.

In moments of stress, try:

- "Let me take a breath and figure out what we know so far..."

- "We'll sort it out—I just need a minute to think."

- "That's frustrating, but here's what I can do right now."

You don't need to fix everything instantly.
You just need to respond with clarity, not chaos.

 Step 4: Solve Problems—Don't Just Spot Them

It's easy to point out issues. It's more valuable to say, "Here's a fix."

Even better? Offer two options.

"This thing's not working—I can either do X or Y. Which would you prefer?"

That's what bosses love. You're not just flagging problems—you're thinking through them. That's promotable energy.

✳️ Step 5: Confidence - Arrogance (and Normies Hate Arrogance)

Confidence says: "I know I bring something to the table."
Arrogance says: "I'm better than everyone else at the table."

You can:

- Speak clearly without dominating

- Accept praise without brushing it off or gloating

- Ask questions without pretending you already know everything

Confidence is calm. Steady. Grounded. It doesn't need to be loud.
And that kind of confidence? It makes people want to work with you—and promote you.

Quick Wins: Promotion-Ready Soft Skills to Practice Now

- Show up 5 minutes early to one thing this week

- Respond to one work message you've been avoiding

- Take a small stressful moment and narrate your calm response (even just to yourself)

- Point out a problem—but offer one helpful solution along with it

- Notice one coworker's good work and give them credit (promotable people uplift others)

People don't get promoted for being perfect.

They get promoted for being reliable, respectful, and easy to work with.

You already have what it takes. These are just the tools to help others see it.

🎯 FINAL WORDS:

You Don't Have to Change Who You Are—Just Learn the Rules

(Or: You're Not Broken, You're Just Underequipped—And That Can Be Fixed)

If you've made it this far, first: you're doing better than you think.

This wasn't a book about perfection. It wasn't a step-by-step manual for becoming the "ideal adult" or some polished professional who never forgets laundry day.

This was a toolkit. A survival guide. A long-overdue, nobody-ever-told-me-this collection of things people are expected to know—but aren't always taught.

You don't have to fake being someone you're not.

You don't have to be loud, polished, extroverted, or hyper-productive to be successful.

But you do need to understand how the game is played—so you can play it on your terms.

🖼 If You Struggle With This Stuff, You're Not Alone

Maybe you missed out on this knowledge because of how you grew up.

Maybe no one ever explained it. Maybe it didn't stick the first few times. Maybe you're neurodivergent, overwhelmed, anxious, or burned out.

You're not lazy. You're not broken. You're not too far behind.

You just need clear info, simple tools, and space to grow at your own pace.

This book was written for you.

What You've Learned Isn't Fancy—It's Foundational

- How to cook without panic

- How to clean a room, keep track of your time, and make peace with your to-do list

- How to budget, build credit, apply for jobs, and talk like a grown-up

- How to speak up, set boundaries, and survive feedback without collapsing

- How to dress, move, email, network, and advocate for yourself with clarity and calm

These are soft skills. Life skills. Core skills.

Not extra. Not optional. Just stuff that makes life work better.

You're Allowed to Start Small

If you don't remember every trick, that's okay.

If you only start with one change, that's okay.

If your first attempt at anything in this book is clumsy, awkward, or full of restarts—that's still progress.

Growth isn't flashy. It's slow. Quiet. Sometimes invisible.

But the fact that you picked up this book, read it, and cared enough to try?

That's powerful.

 You're Allowed to Be Exactly Who You Are— But With Better Tools

You don't have to change your personality. You don't have to squash your quirks.

But learning to manage your time, speak clearly, set boundaries, or build credit?

That's not "selling out."
That's equipping yourself to thrive—so the world sees your best stuff instead of missing it behind a mess of confusion or misunderstanding.

You have value. These tools just help you express it.

✳ So no, you don't have to become
   a different person.

But with the right support?

You can become the version of you that functions, survives, and succeeds—with your dignity and identity intact.

You're not too late. You're not alone. And you've got this.

CAN'T I JUST

Get it Together?

💼 About the Author

Jennifer Larsen writes books for people who are trying—trying to grow, trying to figure things out, trying not to lose it in the grocery store parking lot. She's the founder of Wayfinder Press and the Wayfinder Foundation, where she creates real-world tools that make life a little easier and a lot more human. She believes soft skills are survival skills, and everyone deserves support, no matter how late they're learning.

Also by This Author

Can't I Just Get It Together? is part of the "Can't I Just...?" Collection

Practical books for people figuring it out one day at a time:

- *Can't I Just Stay in My Room?* (Career guide for teens)

- *Can't I Just Skip College?* (Alternatives to traditional college)

- *Can't I Just Help My Kid Pick a Path?* (Parents' guide to careers for teens)

- *Can't I Just Be Like Everyone Else?* (Teen soft skills)

- *Can't I Just Hit Reset?* (Forgiveness for kids)

- *Can't I Just Start Over?* (Forgiveness for teens)

- *Can't I Just Do Something Fun?* (Teen hobbies)

- *Can't I Just Do Something for Me?* (Adult hobbies)

- *Can't I Just Get It Together?* (Adult soft skills) ← you're here

- More on the way.

🤝 About Wayfinder Foundation Inc.

Wayfinder Foundation Inc. is a nonprofit dedicated to helping people build real-life skills, explore meaningful paths, and feel more capable in their day-to-day lives. We create accessible tools, books, and programs for students, parents, educators, and adults—because everyone deserves a roadmap and a little encouragement.

Learn more or support our book donation and outreach efforts at:

🔗 WayfinderFoundationInc.org

www.ingramcontent.com/pod-product-compliance
Lightning Source LLC
Chambersburg PA
CBHW061738120626
46550CB00005B/1826